The Science of Living Things

How do Animals Adapt?

Bobbie Kalman

 Crabtree Publishing Company

The Science of Living Things Series
A Bobbie Kalman Book

For Lesa,
who is right now, as always, so beyond words

Editor-in-Chief
Bobbie Kalman

Writing Team
Bobbie Kalman
John Crossingham

Managing Editor
Lynda Hale

Research
Jacqueline Langille

Editors
Heather Levigne
Kate Calder
Hannelore Sotzek
Niki Walker

Computer Design
Lynda Hale

Production Coordinator
Hannelore Sotzek

Consultant
Patricia Loesche, University of Washington

Photographs
Robert McCaw: pages 19 (top left), 21 (top left), 30, 31 (top)
Photo Researchers, Inc.: Joe B. Blossom: page 9 (top);
    Stephen Dalton: page 27 (top)
Tom Stack & Associates: David B. Fleetham:
    pages 19 (bottom right), 21 (bottom left); Victoria Hurst:
    page 31 (bottom); Kitchin & Hurst: pages 3, 19 (top right);
    Joe and Carol McDonald: page 20 (top); Denise Tackett:
    page 21 (top and bottom right); Roy Toft: page 23 (bottom)
Dave Taylor: page 14
Valan Photos/Fred Bavendam: page 25 (top)
Norbert Wu: page 17 (bottom)
Other images by Digital Stock and Eyewire, Inc.

Illustrations
Barbara Bedell: pages 7, 13, 14, 15, 16 (cats), 17, 28, 29
Antoinette "Cookie" Bortolon: page 10
©Crabtree Publishing Company: page 23
Jeannette McNaughton-Julich: page 6
Bonna Rouse: pages 16 (bottom), 27

Digital Prepress
Embassy Graphics

Printer
Worzalla Publishing Company

Crabtree Publishing Company

PMB 16A
350 Fifth Ave.,
Suite 3308
New York, NY
10118

612 Welland Ave.
St. Catharines,
Ontario,
Canada
L2M 5V6

73 Lime Walk
Headington,
Oxford
OX3 7AD
United Kingdom

Cataloging in Publication Data
Kalman, Bobbie
    How do animals adapt?

(The science of living things)
Includes index.

ISBN 0-86505-980-2 (library bound) ISBN 0-86505-957-8 (pbk.)
This book describes how animals adapt to survive, dicussing camouflage,
mimicry, poisons, defense, adaptations to weather, feeding, and mating.

1. Animals—Adaptation—Juvenile literature. [1. Animals—Adaptation.]
I. Title. II Series: Kalman, Bobbie. Science of living things.

QL49.K294 2000   j591.4   C00-023951
                                                             CIP

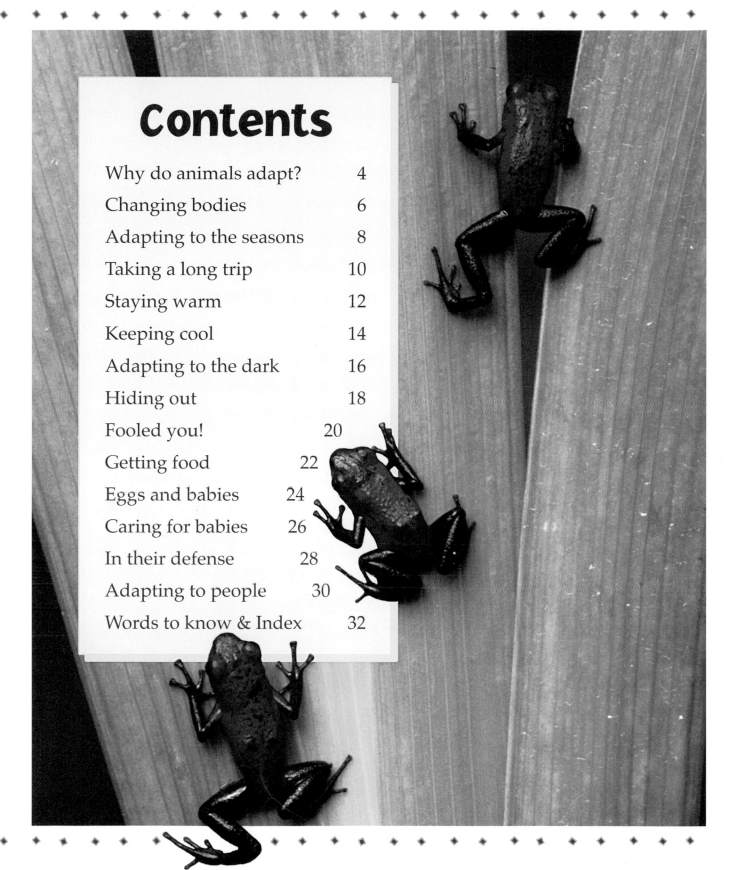

Contents

Why do animals adapt?

The long legs and beak of the ibis allow it to walk into shallow rivers and find food in the riverbed.

The homes of animals are always changing. Some changes happen in nature, and others are caused by people. When an animal's **habitat**, or living area, is no longer the same, that animal must **adapt**, or change, to suit its new habitat.

What is adaptation?

Adaptation occurs in the body of an animal or in the way it behaves. Some adaptations happen quickly, and others take place over millions of years. The way an animal looks or acts today may be very different from the way it looked or behaved long ago.

Adapting to different conditions

Animals adapt to stay alive. They must adapt to find food, escape danger, defend themselves and their young, or adjust their bodies to hot or cold temperatures. Some animals must adapt to losing their habitat and living closer to people. Animal **species**, or types, that cannot adapt to changes in their habitat become **extinct**. An extinct species is one that no longer exists.

A bullfrog's eyes are on the top of its head. This positioning allows the frog to look out for danger without bringing the rest of its body out of the water.

(above) The crocodile is an animal that has remained unchanged for millions of years. Its body is well adapted to its river habitat.

(above) A mountain goat's foot has a hard covering called a **hoof**. Each hoof is split and has a rubbery bottom to give the goat a secure grip on uneven, rocky ground.

(left) Many animals such as horses, dogs, and cats are **domesticated**. These animals depend on people for food and shelter. Some domesticated animals such as cattle have adapted so well to human care that they can no longer survive in the wild.

Changing bodies

All of the animals in a species are not exactly alike. For example, the wolf pups in one litter are of the same species, but each pup can have a slightly different color of fur.

Differences in color and body shape are part of **evolution**. Evolution is a long process during which the body of an animal changes slowly over time. Species are always evolving. Over millions of years, these changes allow the animal to adapt to its habitat.

Adaptation is an important part of evolution. Often an animal is born with changes to its body that give it a better chance of survival than other animals of its species. Changes such as longer legs or larger eyes allow an animal to find more food and live longer than those that have not changed. When animals with these body changes have babies, the changes are passed on to their young. Eventually, the animals with these characteristics become the most common members of the species.

flipper bones

*Sometimes bones give clues about an animal's **ancestor**. The bones in a dolphin's flipper have fingers. Scientists can tell from these fingers that, long ago, the dolphin's ancestor used them to move on land.*

From land to air

Some scientists believe that a few early reptiles evolved into birds. Long ago, the habitat of these reptiles became colder, and the reptiles started growing scales that were similar to feathers to help keep them warm. As their bodies changed and their scales became more feather-like, the reptiles began **gliding** through the air. Their bodies continued to evolve until the animals were able to fly.

Learning to fly

Bats are the only mammals that fly. Their ancestors were small mammals that lived in trees. Over millions of years, these mammals grew flaps of skin on their bodies. They began to glide from one tree to another to find food. Eventually, the bones of their front feet lengthened. The long fingers were covered with thin skin, which formed the bat's wings.

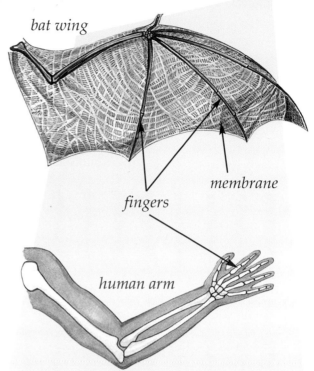

bat wing

membrane

fingers

human arm

Both bats and humans have fingers, but their fingers have different functions. Bats have long fingers that support wings, but human fingers hold objects.

Come on up, the food is great!

Many plant-eating animals, or **herbivores**, compete for food on the **savannah**, or grasslands, of Africa. Most herbivores that live in this habitat feed on long grasses, but giraffes (shown in the picture on the right) have evolved so they can reach leaves on high branches. These leaves contain more nutrients and moisture than grass.

Adapting to the seasons

(above) The fur on a fox's tail is thicker in winter to provide extra warmth and prevent it from freezing.

Some animals live in places that have different seasons. As the seasons change, these animals need to change their body and behavior to cope with the changing **climate** of their home.

A new coat

Animals such as lynxes grow more fur for the cold winter. This fur **insulates** the animals—it keeps their body heat in and the cold out. By spring, the fur becomes too warm and these animals **shed**, or lose, their winter coat.

Winter storage

For many types of animals, finding food in winter is difficult. Some species have learned to **hoard**, or store, extra food for the times when it is not easily available. Squirrels bury nuts in the ground or hide them in trees. Bees collect nectar in the summer and bring it to their hive. They turn the nectar into honey and store it as food for the winter.

You are getting sleepy...

Some animals cannot store or find food during the winter. They go into a type of deep sleep called **hibernation**. Many bears rest for long periods of time. They wake up only three or four times to eat, and then they fall back to sleep until spring.

A few species, such as the dormouse, are **true hibernators**. They do not wake up until winter is over. Their heartbeat and breathing slows down so that the animal uses very little energy and moisture. During hibernation, the animal can survive over six months without eating or drinking.

Brrr! While hibernating, a dormouse's body temperature drops very low to help it save energy.

Animals live off their body fat while they hibernate. When a grizzly bear wakes up in the spring, its body is thin and the animal is ready for a good meal!

Taking a long trip

Another way in which animals adapt to changing seasons is by **migrating**, or traveling from one place to another when the seasons change. Many birds, whales, fish, and deer migrate long distances to a different habitat. Some animals migrate in order to find food or water. Others move to a warmer place because their body is not adapted to survive in a cold climate.

(above) Monarch butterflies migrate up to 3,000 miles (4830 km) each winter to warm places such as Mexico. If they did not migrate, they would freeze to death.

*(top) Geese live and migrate in groups called **flocks**. Being in a large flock helps protect them from enemies.*

Easy riders

Geese make migration easier by flying in a "V" formation, called a **skein**. When the birds at the front of the skein flap their wings, the air pattern they create pulls along the other birds in the formation. The followers do not have to flap as hard because the air supports them. The birds change positions often so the leaders can rest.

Looking for food

Some animals can survive in a cold climate, but they must migrate to find food in winter. Many caribou and reindeer live in the Arctic, where they eat lichen. Lichen does not grow in winter, so the animals must migrate to southern forests to find grasses to eat.

*Not all animals find food in warmer places. Humpback whales migrate to colder waters during part of the year. They go there to feed on tiny sea animals called **krill**.*

It is always warm where these wildebeest live, but sometimes water is difficult to find. When their water source dries up, wildebeest must migrate to find another one.

Staying warm

Some animals have adapted to living in cold places all year. They neither migrate nor hibernate. Instead, their bodies and behaviors have changed to help them keep warm in cold temperatures.

Blubber for warmth

Seals, whales, and walruses all live in cold-water habitats. They have a thick layer of **blubber**, or fat, under their skin that helps keep their body warm. The blubber insulates the body and keeps the cold out.

(above) The blubber of a walrus can be 6 inches (15 cm) thick! It keeps the animal warm in the coldest weather.

(top) A polar bear's fur coat is made up of hollow hairs. Heat from the sun travels through the hairs and into the bear's body. The bear's skin is black to help absorb heat.

The Arctic tundra

Animals that live on the Arctic **tundra** must find ways to keep warm. The tundra is a cold desert and its soil is always frozen. Animals such as musk oxen have a thick fur coat to protect them from the freezing temperatures. Arctic foxes and other small animals dig holes in the snow. The snow traps the heat from their body inside the hole and helps them stay warm.

What tiny ears you have!

Animals lose much of their body heat through their ears. The arctic fox has tiny ears compared to those of its cousin, the red fox. The arctic fox's smaller ears help it keep more heat in its body.

*A penguin's feathers help keep it warm in cold water. The outer feathers are waterproof to keep water away from the penguin's skin. Fluffy feathers called **down** trap warm air between its skin and its outer feathers.*

red fox

arctic fox

The red fox lives in areas with hot summers and cold winters. It needs larger ears to release body heat in summer, whereas the arctic fox needs to hold in heat most of the year.

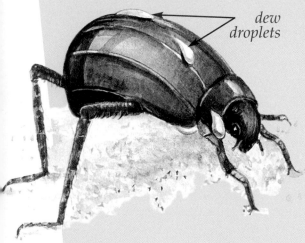

dew droplets

Keeping cool

Deserts are places that receive very little **precipitation**, or rainfall. Few plants grow in deserts because of the hot, dry conditions. Animals in these areas have adapted ways of finding food, storing water, and keeping cool.

Animals that live in dry habitats get most of the water they need from the foods they eat, such as seeds, **succulent** plants, and insects. Some have unusual ways of taking a drink. The darkling beetle drinks water droplets that have formed on its body from the morning dew.

(above) The darkling beetle tilts its body forward and allows the dew droplets on its back to fall into its mouth.

(top) Camels store fat in one or two humps on their back. When they cannot find any water to drink, their body breaks down the fat into water.

Storing water

Deserts do not have ponds or rivers from which animals can drink. In order to survive, desert animals must store as much moisture as possible in their bodies. Nearly all animals release water in their urine, but kangaroo rats have urine that is so dry it is a powder instead of a liquid.

Adapted sleeping habits

Many desert animals hide from the sun during the day. They sleep in a **burrow**, or underground home, in order to stay cool. Desert animals that do not rest in burrows have a low body temperature at night, when it is cool. During the day, their temperature rises slowly. It takes a long time for their bodies to warm up again, so they stay cool during most of the hot day.

Hibernating in the heat

Many deserts are too hot and dry in the summer for some desert animals. Tortoises and toads dig burrows and **estivate** during the hottest, driest months. Estivation is similar to hibernation, but estivating animals go into a deep sleep to escape hot rather than cold conditions. Some animals can estivate up to a year while waiting for rain.

The jerboa digs a burrow in which it estivates during the five hottest months of the year.

The fennec fox lives in the deserts of north Africa. To avoid the hot sun, it spends most of the day in its burrow. The fox's large ears allow heat to escape its body and help it stay cool.

Adapting to the dark

Many animals live in habitats that have little light. Some live in underground caves or in the deep sea. Other animals are **nocturnal**, which means they sleep during the day and are awake at night. Animals that hunt and move in the dark are well adapted to living in their low-light environment.

Echolocation

Most species of bats are nocturnal. They do not need good eyesight to find **prey**, or the animals that they eat. Instead, bats find their way in the dark using **echolocation**. They make high-pitched sounds that travel long distances through the air. When these sounds hit an object in the bat's path, they **echo**, or bounce back. The bat listens to the echo and can tell by the sound whether the object ahead is a tree, rock, or another animal.

*The opening in the center of an eye is called the **pupil**. It controls how much light enters the eye. In bright light, the pupil closes to a narrow opening, preventing animals from being blinded. In dim light, it opens wide, helping an animal see better.*

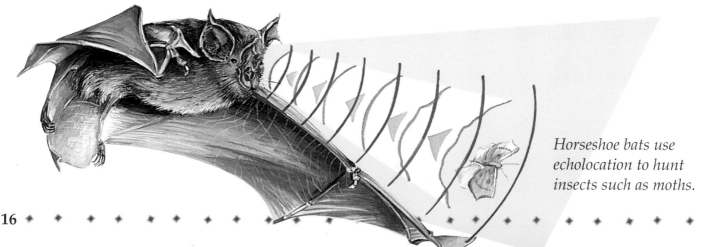

Horseshoe bats use echolocation to hunt insects such as moths.

Singing underwater

Light does not travel well underwater, so many **aquatic**, or water-dwelling, animals cannot see long distances. Dolphins can hunt in dim light using echolocation. Whales such as humpback and fin whales sing songs to stay in contact when they cannot see one another. The humpback whale's song is made up of a series of calls that can travel up to 100 miles (160 km) through water!

No light down here

Many animals live in habitats where there is no light at all. Some animals that live underground are blind, but they have a well-developed sense of touch. The star-nosed mole has sensitive feelers called **tentacles** around its nose. It uses these tentacles to find food and objects in its underground home.

Shine a light

Have you ever wondered why some animals have eyes that can shine in the dark? Many nighttime hunters such as cats and owls have a layer in their eyes called a **tapetum**. The tapetum improves the animal's night vision because any light that hits the tapetum is reflected back onto objects. Sharks also have a tapetum to help them hunt in deep, dark water.

The star-nosed mole can curl its tentacles out of the way when eating or digging underground.

Sharks have developed an excellent sense of smell. This adaptation allows them to smell even the smallest amount of blood from far away. They can follow the scent right to their next meal.

*The ocean depths have little light, so some fish make their own! This viperfish is **bioluminescent**. It has cells along its sides that produce light. It uses its light to attract prey.*

Hiding out

To hide from **predators**, or hunters, many animals have developed **camouflage**. They have markings on their body that allow them to blend in with their habitats. Some animals are so well camouflaged that they are almost impossible to spot. Can you find them on the next page?

Many tundra animals such as this arctic hare have reddish brown fur in the summer. In the winter, however, their fur turns white to blend in with the snow in their habitat.

Plain coat

Some animals rely mainly on their coloring for camouflage. For example, many desert animals have light-brown fur, skin, or feathers to blend in with the sandy landscape. Savannah animals such as gazelles also have light brown coloring. Their color matches the tall golden grass in their habitat.

Spotty coverage

Many animals that live in forests or grasslands have spots or stripes on their fur. These markings look like the shadows created by sunlight shining through long grasses and tall trees. Even an animal as large as a giraffe has spots that hide it from predators.

This ocelot has spots to help it hide among plants while it is hunting.

Find the animals!

(above) The spotted skin of the wood frog blends in so well with these branches that it is almost impossible to spot.

(above) The brown skin of a fringed leaf-tailed gecko helps it hide from enemies on a tree of the same color.

(above) The deadly stonefish is covered in rough scales and spines that camouflage it well among plant-covered rocks.

(right) Most of this shrimp's body is transparent. It appears invisible underwater, making it difficult to spot.

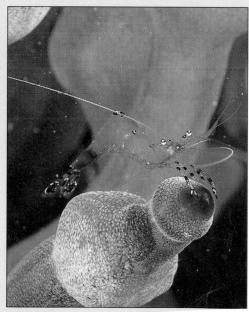

Fooled you!

The tiger swallowtail caterpillar has two eyespots on its rear that make it look like a snake's head. It waves this "head" back and forth to scare predators.

Many animals defend themselves by pretending to be something they are not. When the opossum (above) is threatened, it pretends to be dead! It stays still and breathes very slowly. Most predators eat only live animals, so they leave the opossum alone. Other animals have patterns and shapes that look exactly like something else. This type of camouflage is called **mimicry**. Animals that mimic look like other animals or objects in nature such as leaves or rocks.

(above) This sea horse's body mimics the shape, colors, and texture of the coral in its habitat.

(left) A slender stick insect looks just like a tall blade of grass or twig. When it is not moving, the insect is hard to see.

(above) The feathery growths of the leafy sea dragon look just like seaweed.

(right) Can you see the leaf insect among these leaves? Its brown spots mimic a dying leaf.

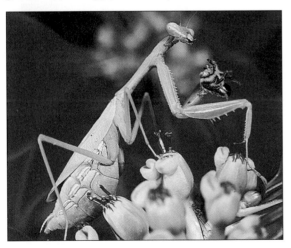

Bison eat mainly grass. They have adapted to this diet by chewing a cud. The animal brings food up from its stomach and chews it again. Its body has a second chance to get more energy from the food.

The praying mantis hunts by waiting silently for smaller insects to come close. When one approaches, the mantis uses its powerful forelimbs to grab the insect.

Getting food

All animals eat other living things to get the energy they need to stay alive. Herbivores get their energy by eating plants. **Carnivores** are animals that receive energy by eating other animals. An animal that eats both plants and animals is called an **omnivore**.

Getting their greens

Grasses, leaves, and other plant parts are difficult for the stomach to **digest**, or break down into energy. Herbivores must grind the plants into small pieces with their teeth so the food can be digested. Some herbivores have wide, flat teeth with sharp ridges for grinding plants.

Matching its prey

Most carnivores hunt for their food. They adapt their behavior according to the type of prey they are hunting. For example, a wolf hunts mice alone because mice have keen hearing, and extra wolves would make too much noise and scare the mice away. When hunting larger prey, wolves roam in groups called **packs**. The wolves in a pack work together to kill strong animals such as caribou.

Seasonal eaters

The giant panda is a type of animal that eats the same **diet**, or type of food, every day. If bamboo was not available, the panda would die. Other animals, such as grizzly bears, have adapted their diet in order to eat the food that is available. In spring, grizzlies eat salmon. In autumn, when the salmon are no longer in the rivers, the bears eat berries.

*(right) Many predators eat only one kind of prey, but not the piranha—it is an **opportunistic feeder**. This tiny fish attacks and eats anything that moves!*

Tool users

When we eat, we use tools such as knives and forks. Some animals have also learned how to use objects to help them find or eat their food.

The Egyptian vulture sometimes uses rocks as eating tools. This bird likes to eat eggs, which it cracks by dropping them. When it finds a heavy ostrich egg, however, it cannot lift it with its beak. Instead, it picks up a rock to drop on the egg in order to break it.

Chimpanzees like to eat termites, but their fingers are too big to fit into the small holes of termite homes. To reach the termites, a chimpanzee strips the leaves off a twig and pokes it into the hole of a termite nest. The termites attack the twig and hang onto it. The chimp removes the twig from the hole with the termites attached and licks them off the twig.

Eggs and babies

Animals must **reproduce**, or make babies. Many male animals have calls, dances, or markings to help them attract a female partner. In nature, the strongest, healthiest animals have the best chance of surviving. Scientists think that many male animals must prove their good health to a female before she will mate with them.

Male bighorn sheep (shown above) charge at one another to prove their worth. Some lizards stand on their back legs and grab their opponents around the middle. This challenging behavior ensures that the strongest male makes more babies. If the father is strong, chances are good that his babies will also be strong.

Egg-laying animals

Amphibians, birds, insects, fish, and reptiles all lay eggs that contain their young. Many animals feed on these eggs, however. Some birds and reptiles guard their eggs and young, but other animals do not. Frogs and fish lay thousands of eggs at a time to make sure that at least a few of their young will survive.

Ready when you are

Kangaroos live in a dry habitat. Their young, called **joeys**, need a good supply of water to grow up healthy. Female kangaroos are adapted to giving birth only when water is available. After kangaroos mate, the female stores the egg inside her body. The egg, however, does not **gestate**, or continue to grow, until there is enough water available to support the joey.

On to warmer waters

Many whales, such as humpback and blue whales, feed in cold ocean waters. When it is time to give birth, they migrate toward warmer water. Scientists believe that the water of the feeding grounds is too cold and rough for the young whale calves to survive.

(above) Many male birds rely on their bright feathers to impress a female. This male frigate bird inflates its red chest to attract a mate.

(right) A mother kangaroo cares for two joeys at once—a newborn and an older one. Her body makes two different kinds of milk to feed each joey.

Caring for babies

Caring for babies after they are born is a difficult job for animals. Even the crocodile must protect its young from predators. Parents have many ways of protecting their babies. Some babies can even protect themselves!

A few species of animals have adapted to sharing the work of raising young. Some female ducks leave their ducklings in a group called a **crèche**. While one female looks for food, the other females stay behind and guard the ducklings.

*Unlike many animals, Canada geese often live with one mate during their whole life. Both parents care for their young, called **goslings**.*

Here, you take it!

Some cuckoos give the work of raising their young to other types of birds. A female cuckoo finds several nests—one for each of her eggs. She waits until the owners leave their nest, and then she lays an egg. Sometimes her egg looks similar to those already in the nest. When the cuckoo chick hatches, it pushes the other eggs or chicks out of the nest.

I can walk!

Most mammals give birth to **live young** that can walk and follow their parents soon after birth. A baby wildebeest can walk five minutes after it is born. It can keep up with the rest of the herd when searching for food and water or changing location to avoid predators.

This cuckoo chick is already twice the size of the adult sparrow, but the sparrow continues to feed it every day, treating it as her own.

*Spiders have many young at one time, but the babies cannot all live in the same area. The young spiders find a place to live by **ballooning**. They raise their **abdomen**, or rear, spin a long strand of silk, and let the breeze carry them to a new home.*

Many sea lions live on beaches in huge groups. Each sea lion pup has its own special scent. Mothers use their excellent sense of smell to locate their pups in a crowd.

In their defense

Some animals need more protection than others. Many slow, timid animals have developed special defenses because they are too slow to escape their attackers. Their bodies are protected by armor, sharp spines, poisons, bad odors, or explosives!

*The porcupine's **quills** are very dangerous. They can stay in a predator's skin for weeks and even cause death.*

Ouch!

Hedgehogs and echidnas use sharp spikes for protection. Their spines are short and cover the animal's back. If these animals feel afraid, they roll themselves into a spiky ball. The porcupine fish is another animal with spines. When threatened, this fish sucks in water to expand its body and raise the sharp spines that cover it. Most predators stay away from spiny creatures because they are too dangerous to eat.

Body armor

Turtles, tortoises, and snails have hard shells for defense. If attacked, they can pull their head and limbs into their protective shell. Armadillos also have tough plates on their back and sides, but they do not pull their limbs into a shell. Like the hedgehog, they roll into a ball when they are threatened.

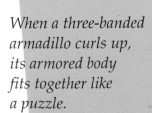

When a three-banded armadillo curls up, its armored body fits together like a puzzle.

Chemical warfare

Many animals make poisons in their body. Some, such as snakes and spiders, use poison to hunt. Many frogs and other amphibians have poison in their skin that they release when a predator grabs them. Cane toads squirt a liquid out of large **glands** on the back of their head! Their enemy spits them out when it tastes the terrible poison.

Bad perfume

A skunk makes an awful-smelling fluid called **musk** to keep enemies away. When threatened, it shoots the musk at an enemy from a gland in its rear. The musk not only smells bad, but it also blinds an animal that is sprayed in the eyes.

Say it, don't spray it!

Many snakes such as vipers and rattlesnakes use a poisonous bite for hunting and protection. Their poison, called **venom**, is injected into animals through sharp front teeth called **fangs**. The spitting cobra can shoot its venom at an attacker!

(above) This sea slug eats poisonous sea anemones, but the sea anemone's poison cells do not harm the slug. The slug can even use these cells to protect itself. An animal that bites one of the slug's hairlike growths gets a dose of the anemone's poison.

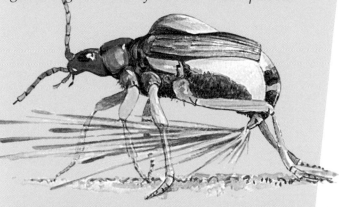

The bombardier beetle produces two chemicals in its body. When it is threatened, it mixes these two chemicals in its abdomen. The mixture creates a hot explosion that the beetle can shoot at its enemy. The beetle aims by pointing its abdomen at a predator.

Adapting to people

Instead of adapting themselves, humans change their surroundings to suit their needs. When people build a city or clear land for farming, they destroy the habitats of many animal species. Often, the animals cannot adapt to their new surroundings. They must find another place to live. Some animal species face extinction because they have lost their habitat and source of food.

Not all animals are endangered by the changes. A few species have found ways to adapt to the new habitats that humans create. Omnivores such as coyotes and bears adapt by finding new sources of food in or near cities. These animals survive by eating food they find at garbage dumps. At night, raccoons (shown above) travel into the city streets and people's back yards and find their food in garbage cans.

New homes

When an animal's habitat is taken away, it will try to find the next best thing. Sometimes skunks live beneath people's porches or homes. Bobcats have also been found living in towns. Some alligators have made a second home in canals, golf courses, and swimming pools!

This will do nicely

Animals that live in trees or on rocky cliffs adapt well to living on buildings and other structures that people have made. In the wild, pigeons often nest on cliffs, but in cities they make nests on the edges of buildings.

What if they cannot adapt?

Many animals cannot adapt fast enough when humans destroy their habitat. If an animal loses its home or its source of food and cannot adapt, it will die. Many species become extinct. Wildlife organizations all over the world work hard to keep animals from losing their homes. **Sanctuaries**, or protected areas in the wild, help save many species from extinction.

As cities get larger, deer are forced to graze in new areas such as a back yard. Since cities have few predators, the number of deer in the area increases.

The coyote's strong sense of smell helps it find a meal in the garbage people throw away.

Words to know

amphibian An animal that begins life in the water and then lives on land as an adult

ancestor An animal from which similar animals have descended

bioluminescent Describing an animal's ability to produce its own light

camouflage A color pattern on an animal that allows it to hide from enemies

climate The normal, long-term weather conditions for an area

echolocation An animal's ability to find its way around by sending and receiving sounds

estivate To be in an inactive state during the summer to avoid extremely hot conditions

evolve To change or develop slowly over time

extinct Describing an animal or plant species that no longer exists

gestate To grow inside the mother's body

gland A body part that releases a substance, such as a liquid

hibernate To be in an inactive state during the winter to avoid extremely cold conditions

insulate To cover with material that stops heat from leaving the body

live young Describing a baby animal that does not hatch from an egg

migrate To move from one location to another in order to mate or find food or water

mimicry A color pattern or growth that makes an animal look like something else in nature

species A group of closely related living things that can have babies

succulent Describing a plant or leaf that contains large amounts of water, such as a cactus

Index

1 2 3 4 5 6 7 8 9 0   Printed in the U.S.A.   9 8 7 6 5 4 3 2 1 0